LIVING WITH DEATH

SHY HOUSTON

Published by SHY HOUSTON, 2024.

Living With Death

*A Comprehensive Guide to
Embracing Mortality*

Shy Houston

© Copyright 2024 - All rights reserved.

The content contained within this book may not be reproduced, duplicated or transmitted without direct written permission from the author or the publisher.

Under no circumstances will any blame or legal responsibility be held against the publisher, or author, for any damages, reparation, or monetary loss due to the information contained within this book, either directly or indirectly.

<u>Legal Notice:</u>

This book is copyright protected. It is only for personal use. You cannot amend, distribute, sell, use, quote or paraphrase any part, or the content within this book, without the consent of the author or publisher.

<u>Disclaimer Notice:</u>

Please note the information contained within this document is for educational and entertainment purposes only. All effort has been executed to present accurate, up to date, reliable, complete information. No warranties of any kind are declared or implied. Readers acknowledge that the author is not engaged in the rendering of legal, financial, medical or professional advice. The content within this book has been derived from various sources. Please consult a licensed professional before attempting any techniques outlined in this book.

By reading this document, the reader agrees that under no circumstances is the author responsible for any losses, direct or indirect, that are incurred as a result of the use of the information contained within this document, including, but not limited to, errors, omissions, or inaccuracies.

Introduction

Acknowledging mortality is the first step.

We all journey through life along a winding path, filled with both challenges and joys, steadily progressing toward the inevitable crossroads of death. As Isaac Asimov wisely noted, "Life is pleasant. Death is peaceful. It's the transition that's troublesome" (*Isaac Asimov Quotes*, n.d.). In this comprehensive guide, we embark on a quest to unravel the intricate relationship between life and death, exploring scientific and spiritual perspectives. It's important to note, however, that our focus isn't fixated on the daunting transition but on comprehending it, appreciating it, and finding serenity in the face of the inevitable.

If we delve into the very essence of life, we find it marked by the first breath we take, concluding with the inevitability of death. It's a natural, ever-present aspect of our existence, much like the two sides of a well-loved coin. Creation and destruction coexist, akin to the dance between life and death. However, the challenge arises when we grapple with the fear instilled by our understanding of these intricacies. This fear can be paralyzing, clouding various aspects of our lives. Within this book, you'll discover ways to make peace with the end of life, learning to live wholeheartedly and mindfully, embracing the joys, triumphs, and setbacks without allowing the impending end to distract you from savoring every moment.

We embark on a journey to unravel the threads of mortality, not solely through philosophy but also with a scientific understanding. Through the lens of science, we find proof and perspective on mortality. Insights from biologists guide us to understand life as a complex arrangement of molecular structures and cells, programmed to reproduce and eventually disintegrate. While this may sound daunting, we're reminded that we are blessed creatures with more than just a biological existence; we possess a spirit within. Spirituality adds another layer to our understanding, offering beliefs in concepts like reincarnation or an afterlife and providing reassurance and hope beyond the finality of death.

Debunking the gloomy perception of death, we emphasize that mortality doesn't have to be a daunting thought. A shift in mindset, accepting our mortality, leads to personal growth, happiness, confidence, and lasting peace. For those struggling with the fear of death, spiritual leader Eckhart Tolle advises, "Die before you die," urging us to let go of physical and egoistic attachments to achieve spiritual liberation while still alive (*A Quote from the Power of Now*, n.d.).

Life is more than a waiting game for the end; it's about understanding your fragility, acknowledging your mortality, and appreciating the profound beauty encountered throughout your lifespan. Life and death are more than meets the eye; it's an internal exploration, realizing the power to shape a meaningful life and leave a lasting legacy. Take that first step to explore, learn, and understand that life can be more than just existing; it can be about loving and empowering yourself to live a fulfilling and enriching life.

Chapter 1: Understanding Death in Today's World

The fabric of life changes over time, tying together complex strands of happiness, difficulties, and grief. However, these threads frequently lose their once-valued significance in today's fast-paced world. Time elapses as we pursue our objectives and aspirations, leaving little time to fully appreciate each moment. This chapter explores the complexities surrounding mortality by looking at various spiritual perspectives, cultural viewpoints, and psychological aspects that all work together to shape our understanding of this universal phenomenon.

Cultural Perspectives and Spiritual Diversification on Death and Dying

Spirituality continues to be a crucial component of our investigation of life and death, even in this day of sophisticated technology and information. Why? It serves as a lens that provides distinct frameworks for understanding life, death, and the afterlife. It deepens our understanding of death, whether we are thinking about the cyclical nature of existence in Eastern philosophies or the idea of eternal life in Western traditions.

Cultural Beliefs

Examining diverse cultural perspectives on death and dying reveals a treasure trove of rituals, ceremonies, and beliefs. Every culture adds its own perspective, which helps to develop both a more expansive perspective and an appreciation for the richness inherent in our differences. Christianity sees death as a transition to an afterlife, either with God in heaven or, unfortunately, in hell, based on one's earthly deeds. Islam envisions an afterlife and Judgment Day, with death marking the transition to paradise or accountability for one's actions. Hinduism embraces the belief in reincarnation or Samsara, where death is a transition to a new life based on past actions. Buddhism shares a similar view of reincarnation, creating a continuous cycle of birth, death, and rebirth. Judaism sees death as a natural part of life, focusing on how one lives in the present. Other traditional beliefs also view death as a transition to an ancestral or spirit world.

Cultures worldwide, despite their differences, converge on the singular belief that life on Earth is a transition to a spiritual realm or world. This idea crosses over into the scientific sphere from the spiritual and philosophical spheres.

Science and Death

The significance of striking a balance between spiritual beliefs and scientific understanding is emphasized by Albert Einstein's words, "Science without religion is lame; religion without science is blind" (*Albert Einstein Quotes*, n.d.). While science provides knowledge about the physical aspect of death, spirituality offers comfort and hope in the face of this unavoidable reality. Acknowledging our mortality is the first step in dispelling the fear associated with it. Integrating spirituality into our lives becomes crucial, providing peace and comfort during moments of both joy and grief.

Science tells us that our bodies will be born; cells will thrive, multiply, and then die. But spirituality tells us how to live, what to do and not do, and finally, what happens to us even after death.

Psychological Aspects of Mortality

Facing our deepest fears and anxieties is a necessary step toward acknowledging our mortality. To achieve personal development and long-lasting peace, this path necessitates reflection, comprehension, and the destruction of fear's foundations. A few key ideas and methods to navigate these psychological foundations include:

- Death is an integral part of life's natural cycle.

- Acknowledge, understand, and then accept mortality.

- Spiritual beliefs shape how you perceive mortality, dispelling the fear associated with mortality.

- Integrating spirituality into daily routines helps as a coping mechanism.

To put the above into practice, start with simple techniques that will help you build a mindful mindset.

To achieve mindfulness, you can start gradually.

- Find a quiet space where you can sit down comfortably.

- Close your eyes and take a few deep breaths as you center yourself.

- Focus your attention on your breathing.

- Feel the sensation of each breath coming in and going out.

- When your thoughts begin to wander, gently bring your attention back to your breath without any judgment.

- Slowly expand your awareness of your surroundings as you appreciate the sights, sounds, and sensations in the present moment.

From here, you will need to cultivate compassion. This will allow you to find a sense of purpose and also realize one simple truth: we are all walking the same path and the end is the same, but what we do with our time is what makes it all worth it or not.

- Try to identify any opportunity that you could use to help someone; it could either be a small gesture or a larger act of kindness.

- Approach the situation with an open heart and a willingness to make a positive impact.

- Consider the shared humanity that connects us all.

- Recognize that everyone has struggles and good times.

- Perform the act of kindness, whether it's offering a helping hand, kind words, or a thoughtful gesture.

- Reflect on the experience and notice how it contributes to a sense of purpose and connection for you.

Seeking spiritual enlightenment comes last, as you will now have the ability to experience and be aware of every moment, no longer stuck in your thoughts. You will have also achieved a goal or purpose for your life. This makes your life more real. With spirituality, you obtain a master key that will propel you forward. You get to find reassurance and understanding of the unknown. You will no longer fear it but embrace the future.

- Start by taking some time for self-reflection and exploration.

- You could choose any resource, like a book or video, that delves into different cultural perspectives on spirituality and depth and engage with the material with an open mind as you absorb the wisdom shared.

● Do not judge anything you discover.

● Consider incorporating some of the elements you come across into your daily life during your spiritual journey.

*****

We explored how different cultures and beliefs shape our understanding of life and death. From science to spirituality, there's a common message: Life extends beyond the physical. Recognizing our own mortality gives us the ability to turn fear into understanding and make sure that our journey is not just traveled but meaningfully lived.

Now, we move to the next chapter, diving into accepting death. It's about finding meaning and navigating life's impermanence.

Chapter 2: Embracing the Inevitability of Death

Imagine for a moment that we were invincible, immortal, and eternal. Sounds intriguing, right? Well, not really. Without the ticking of time, we'd lose the essence of valuing, appreciating, and looking forward to anything. Life would become a dull, pointless cycle, devoid of morals, judgment, and purpose, leaving us aimless and weak in the face of a pointless existence. Oddly enough, it's death that gives our lives meaning, making it an inevitable part of our journey.

Shifting Our Perspective and Seeing Death as a Part of Life

From our very first understanding of life, we grasp the inevitable reality of death. This realization isn't a lesson saved for adulthood; it's woven into our childhood experiences—the death of a pet, an insect, or a loved one. Knowing that life isn't infinite adds depth and peace to our existence. Life's journey, with its highs and lows, gains significance because of its impermanence. Each moment becomes precious as mortality compels us to value and appreciate the little things. Even when we look back across history and cultures, from Egyptian pyramids to Greek beliefs, death has been revered, emphasizing its integral role in the fabric of life.

Building Acceptance by Letting Go of Fear and Denial

Understanding that death is not our enemy but a shared fate for all living beings brings a sense of peace. Acceptance allows us to release anxiety and fears beyond our control. If we could control life and live forever, death might be a foe. Yet, as part of the natural order, there's nothing to fear, for we know its inevitability. Embracing this reality frees us from denial and fear, allowing us to live fully in the present.

Valuing our fleeting time on Earth means every passing second becomes an opportunity to make it worthwhile. Seeking experiences, forming bonds, and pursuing passions contribute to a positive lifestyle. Scientific studies affirm the wisdom of embracing our mortality and fostering a hopeful, anxiety-free life. In understanding and accepting death, we find the key to living a life that is not just long but truly fulfilling.

Preparing for the End with Practical Considerations

Practical considerations can give one a sense of control and preparedness when facing the inevitable end. Even though we cannot foresee every scenario, having a plan in place can help our loved ones cope.

It can be difficult to start a conversation about end-of-life preferences, such as funeral plans and healthcare directives, and we will look into this later on, but doing so guarantees that our desires are honored.

Properly planning for life for those close to us after our deaths helps ensure a smooth transition. Acknowledging the practical aspects of our journey's end allows us to leave a thoughtful legacy and grant peace of mind to ourselves and our loved ones.

Living with Grief

Our fear of dying is not the only source of anxiety. We care about other people and, of course, we would not want them to pass away. However, grief is an unavoidable traveling companion that serves as a moving reminder of the depth of our relationships.

Even though grieving is incredibly difficult, there are coping strategies that can make things easier.

- Expressing emotions through open communication with friends, family, or support groups fosters healing.

- Understanding that grief has its own timeline allows for patience and self-compassion.

- Engaging in activities that bring solace and maintaining routines offer stability amid the storm. Embracing the memories of those we've lost becomes a source of strength, transforming grief into a testament of enduring love.

Coping with loss is an ongoing process, but with time and support, it becomes a journey toward resilience and acceptance.

Finding Peace in Mortality

To find peace in our mortality is to accept that death is inevitable. Rather than taking away from life's vibrancy, acceptance increases our gratitude for each moment. The insight is in realizing that life is a transitory gift, with mortality serving as the paintbrush that adds dimension.

Developing thankfulness for the encounters, connections, and chances life offers opens the door to inner tranquility. A sense of fulfillment is derived from accepting the present moment, engaging in mindfulness exercises, and realizing our interconnectedness with all living things. It is about bringing our viewpoints into harmony with the cycles of life, accepting that life is transitory, and realizing that death is not a blank slate but rather the beginning of something new.

Accepting the inevitable is a powerful decision that gives us a deep sense of peace and enables us to appreciate the splendor of our fleeting lives.

Easy Steps to a More Fulfilled Life

Are you wondering how to embrace your own mortality? It's simpler than you think:

- Live mindfully, letting go of regrets from the past and anxieties about the future. Being mindful helps you stay in the now and gives each moment greater significance.

- Break the taboo by having open discussions about death. By promoting acceptance and removing fear, normalizing discussions about death helps it become a part of life.

- Follow your passions with all of your might, because time is limited. Dreams should be pursued quickly because they give us a sense of fulfillment and purpose when we realize we have a limited amount of time.

- Make peace with the past by resolving unresolved issues and giving generous forgiveness. You are free to fully embrace the present when you make peace with past hurts.

- Spend time with those you love; relationships are life's real treasures. Treasure the times spent with those you love, as these relationships enhance our lives in ways that nothing else can.

Living truly, building relationships, and appreciating each day are all part of accepting your mortality. These easy steps give your journey depth and purpose, extending and improving the quality of your life.

*****

Embracing mortality enhances life's vibrancy. From acknowledging death's role to navigating grief and finding peace, the journey is profound. Live fully, cherish relationships, and savor each fleeting moment. Now, get ready for the next chapter, where we look into religion and spirituality more deeply.

Chapter 3: The Role of Faith and Spirituality in Understanding Mortality

Understanding death is an intricate journey that often intersects with faith and spirituality, guiding individuals through the labyrinth of existential questions. In this chapter, we navigate the diverse perspectives offered by different religions, exploring how belief systems not only provide comfort but also converge in their underlying messages about mortality. We delve into the intricacies of finding solace, forming connections with the divine, and the universal themes that bridge the gap between various faiths.

Exploring Different Religious Views on Death

Every religion presents a distinctive narrative about death, shaping the way its followers perceive the inevitable end of life. Take Buddhism, for instance, with its teachings on impermanence and the cyclical nature of existence through concepts like reincarnation. In contrast, Christianity's emphasis on an afterlife and the promise of eternal peace resonates deeply with its followers. By examining these varied perspectives, we not only acknowledge the richness of human beliefs but also find common threads that unite us in our contemplation of mortality.

Finding Comfort in Belief Systems

One of the remarkable aspects of faith is its ability to provide solace amid the uncertainties of life and death. Rituals, prayers, and the overarching belief in a higher purpose contribute to the emotional support systems embedded in various religions. The familiarity of religious practices offers stability during times of turbulence, acting as pillars of strength for anyone navigating the inevitable journey toward the end of life.

Divine Connections

The concept of a higher power plays a significant role in how we cope with mortality. Whether through prayer, meditation, or other spiritual practices, the quest for a divine connection often becomes a profound source of peace and reassurance. These connections, unique to each faith, serve as rays of hope, illuminating the path through the existential darkness.

Death in the Real World

To deepen our understanding, we turn to the wisdom of faith leaders spanning the globe. Their experiences and teachings provide valuable insights into navigating the complexities of mortality. Through poignant anecdotes and profound teachings, we gain a human perspective on how faith serves as a guiding light in the face of the unknown.

In this exploration of faith and mortality, let us draw inspiration from two remarkable stories.

Story from Rabbi Miriam Cohen, Jerusalem, Israel

Rabbi Miriam reflected on a moment of profound connection during a time of grief in her community. In the face of loss, she witnessed individuals from diverse backgrounds coming together, transcending religious boundaries, to offer solace and support. Through this shared humanity, Rabbi Miriam's story highlights how faith, regardless of specific doctrines, unites people in the pursuit of compassion and understanding amid the challenges of mortality.

Story from Swami Rajananda, Rishikesh, India

Swami Rajananda recounted a transformative journey of self-discovery and mortality awareness through the lens of Hindu philosophy. He shared the wisdom of embracing life's impermanence, drawing parallels with the Buddhist concept of impermanence. Swami Rajananda emphasized that, despite the apparent differences in religious doctrines, the underlying essence of finding purpose and transcendence resonates universally. His narrative exemplifies the interconnectedness of faiths and their shared pursuit of meaning in the face of mortality.

These stories from faith leaders underscore the universal themes that bind us, transcending cultural and doctrinal boundaries as we collectively seek understanding and comfort in the intricate tapestry of life and death.

The Universality of Religious Conclusions

While the surface of religious doctrines may seem divergent, a closer examination reveals striking similarities in the fundamental messages they convey about life and death. Under cultural and doctrinal diversity, there is a shared human quest for meaning, purpose, and transcendence. From the Buddhist acceptance of impermanence to the Christian hope for an afterlife, these varied paths converge on the universal theme of seeking understanding and comfort in the face of mortality.

*****

In conclusion, exploring the diverse perspectives of faith and spirituality, we have looked into not only the intricacies of individual belief systems but also the common ground that unites us in our search for meaning on this shared journey through life and death.

Chapter 4: Living Fully Despite Mortality

As we explore living fully in spite of the limitations imposed by our mortal nature, we come across transforming practices that enable us to embrace each moment, find joy in the face of uncertainty, and cultivate resilience in the face of life's challenges.

Fully Present in Each Moment

The practice of mindfulness, or fully focusing on the present moment, is the foundation of our journey. This tenet shifts our attention away from regrets from the past and worries about the future, enabling us to fully appreciate the richness of the present moment. Being mindful fosters an appreciation for the inherent beauty in every breath, every sight, and every interaction, rather than trying to change the past or forecast the future.

Gaining mastery over mindfulness weaves moments together to create a life that is genuinely fulfilling.

Cultivating Joy Amid Life's Unpredictability

The journey of life is inherently uncertain, and accepting this fact enables us to find joy despite unforeseen events. To cultivate joy means to acknowledge that happiness is an internal state of being rather than something that is purely dependent on circumstances outside of oneself. The capacity to find joy in small pleasures becomes an effective tool, whether in times of celebration or when facing life's obstacles.

Accepting that life is temporary enables us to find joy, laughter, and beauty in the ups and downs of our path.

Building Resilience in the Face of Life's Challenges

Resilience emerges as our unwavering ally when faced with adversity, which is an inevitable companion on life's journey. Recognizing setbacks as a normal part of life is a necessary step in building resilience. We learn to see challenges as chances for growth rather than as insurmountable roadblocks. Resilience is the ability to overcome adversity and come out stronger and wiser, not to avoid it. By developing a resilient mindset, we can turn adversity into a force for personal growth and strengthen our capacity to face mortality's uncertainties with bravery and grace.

Weaving Mindfulness, Joy, and Resilience

Looking into the threads that make up life, observing people's thoughts and what leads them to fear death and what leads them to eventually overcome the end of life and actually live their life to its best potential, we find that this is possible by merging the threads of mindfulness, joy, and resilience. This ultimately leads to acceptance.

We can navigate the complexities of our existence with purpose and vigor when we learn to embrace each moment, find joy in the midst of uncertainty, and develop resilience in the face of adversity. The path to living fully is a celebration of the time we have and the richness each moment has to offer, not an attempt to avoid death.

The Relationship Between Mindfulness, Joy, Acceptance, Resilience, and Death

If you're wondering what's so great about being able to accept death as a natural part of life and not succumb to the idea that there is no reason to go on since everything will end anyway, well, that's not true. There is more to life when you learn to let go of this idea.

For one, an awareness of our mortality serves as a compass, guiding us toward choices that lead to fewer regrets. The knowledge that our time is limited motivates us to give priority to the things that really matter, which helps us make decisions and take actions with meaning.

There's something known as the death positivity movement, which encourages an open and honest conversation about the inevitable end of life. By removing the stigma surrounding death, people can engage in discussions that bring about understanding, acceptance, and a more profound connection with our mortality.

By including death in mindfulness exercises, we accept that it exists and is a part of life. We can develop a deeper understanding of death through death meditation, which enhances our appreciation of the present and brings about a deep sense of clarity and gratitude.

A lot of successful people say they use the fear of dying as a strong motivator. People are inspired to follow their passions, take chances, and make the most of their time when they realize how fleeting life is. The sense of urgency brought about by death becomes the motivation behind significant achievements.

Thinking back on the art of living life to the fullest in spite of death, we see that these practices go beyond satisfaction of the ego. They create empathy, understanding, and a common joy of life, which have an impact on our society as a whole. Accepting fullness is an affirmation of the deep beauty woven into the fabric of existence rather than a denial of mortality.

So, immerse yourself fully in the present moment, appreciating the beauty in each breath, sight, and experience. Find happiness in simple pleasures, recognizing that joy is an internal state of being, independent of external circumstances. View challenges as opportunities for growth, bouncing back stronger and wiser in the face of adversity.

Mortality awareness is vital as it serves as a guide, encouraging decisions that lead to fewer regrets. Always join the death positivity movement, fostering honest discussions about the inevitable end of life. Meditate on death within mindfulness practices, deepening your understanding and gratitude for the present moment. Lastly, allow the awareness of life's impermanence to propel you toward meaningful accomplishments and a purposeful existence.

*****

To conclude, by embracing these principles, we not only enrich our individual lives but also contribute to the collective tapestry of human experience. As we continue our journey, may the intertwining threads of mindfulness, joy, and resilience guide us toward a fuller, more meaningful existence.

Chapter 5: Life's Purpose Knowing Our Mortal Nature

We discover the deep significance of defining values, cultivating meaningful relationships, and leaving a lasting legacy—making our mark on the complex tapestry of existence—as we investigate life's purpose in the midst of our mortal nature.

Identifying Your Values and Priorities

Deep reflection on our priorities and values is the first step toward realizing the purpose of our lives. Because we are mortal and time is limited, it is important to determine what is really important. Finding our core values gives us a compass to help us make decisions in life and makes sure that what we do is in line with our innermost beliefs. We embrace a sense of urgency to give priority to experiences, relationships, and projects that align with our values as a result of realizing our mortality, which enhances our journey by giving it meaning and fulfillment.

Creating Meaningful Relationships

Meaningful relationships are an integral part of living a purposeful life. The significance of establishing relationships that go beyond surface-level interactions is highlighted by our mortal nature. Death is a poignant reminder that the depth of our lives is determined by the caliber of our relationships. It becomes essential to devote time and effort to creating real connections because these bonds enhance our sense of identity, offer emotional support, and serve as a constant source of happiness when faced with life's uncertainties.

Making Your Mark and Leaving a Legacy

Because we are mortal, the idea of a legacy becomes extremely important. Determining one's purpose in life becomes inextricably linked to making an impact on the world. Legacy includes our influence on other people and the environment, not just our major accomplishments. Since we are all mortal, it is imperative that we take into account the imprints we leave behind, including the values we instill, the positive change we inspire, and the contributions we make to the well-being of others. Through the deliberate shaping of our choices and actions, we leave a legacy that endures beyond our mortal lives, transcending the confines of time.

Within Being

So far, we have navigated the three interrelated facets of finding our life's purpose: defining our values, cultivating deep connections with others, and leaving a lasting legacy. Each component, when combined, makes a tapestry that symbolizes the singularity of our mortal journey. Life's purpose is a real, practical question that arises from our realization of life's transience, rather than an abstract philosophical thought. On the other hand, the search for meaning in life is not over. There is more.

The Essence of Values

Values are guiding concepts that light our way and direct our decisions and deeds. Determining our values is a continuous process that is impacted by experiences, introspection, and accepting our mortality. We bring authenticity and depth to our lives when we live according to our values.

The Strength of Bonds

A meaningful life revolves around meaningful relationships. Our mortality forces us to invest in relationships that provide happiness, support, and a sense of common humanity rather than settle for flimsy ones. These connections, which are based on sincerity and trust, give us comfort and strength and enhance our mortal journey.

Legacy Beyond Time

Leaving a legacy is a way for us to acknowledge the influence we have on the people and world around us. Our mortality forces us to reflect on the enduring effects we have, how our deeds affect other people's lives, and the positive transformation we bring about. When we intentionally leave a legacy, we make sure that our impact goes beyond the limited time we have on this planet.

So, what have you discovered?

- Think back on the values that best represent your identity and serve as a guide for your choices and behavior.

- Spend time and effort cultivating relationships that enrich and uplift your life.

- Strive to mold your behavior in a way that will benefit others long after you pass away.

- Accept the urgency of dying in order to live a life that is true to yourself and has meaning.

*****

The interplay of values, relationships, and legacy becomes the compass as we make our way through the complex terrain of life's purpose. Our mortality ceases to be a constraint and instead acts as a motivator, inspiring us to live life with meaning, love profoundly, and leave a lasting legacy. We discover meaning that resonates throughout the fabric of existence when we embrace the purpose of life, which is woven into the fabric of our mortality.

Chapter 6: Health, Wellness, and Longevity

Now that we have reached the halfway point, let us explore the fountain of youth and discover the keys to good health, happiness, and winning the long game on this life-changing roller coaster. We examine the fundamentals that lead to a strong and long life, from developing healthy habits to maintaining mental clarity and taking preventative action against serious illnesses.

Healthy Habits for a Long Life

Let us start by discussing how to lay the groundwork for a lengthy and prosperous journey during this exciting adventure. You are familiar with the routine.

- Mix up your workouts by incorporating strength, flexibility, and aerobic training.

- Eat a varied, nutrient-dense diet that prioritizes whole grains, fruits, vegetables, lean proteins, and other nutrients.

- Make sure you are getting enough water for your body's needs and general health.

- For the sake of your physical and emotional health, try to get between seven and nine hours of good sleep every night.

- Engage in stress-reduction practices like yoga, deep breathing, and meditation.

- Moderate alcohol consumption can improve general health.

- Avoid smoking for the sake of your heart and lungs.

- Plan regular physical examinations and screenings to identify possible problems early.

Mental Health Awareness: Maintaining Mental Acuity

Now, let's shift gears to the powerhouse—your noggin. Mental health is the rock star of the show. Keep that brain flexin' and sharp by giving it a workout.

- Take part in mental-stirring activities like games, puzzles, and picking up new abilities.

- For both emotional and cognitive health, getting enough sleep is essential.

- Utilize mindfulness, relaxation methods, and support-seeking strategies to manage stress.

- To fight loneliness and improve cognitive function, continue to engage in meaningful social interactions.

- Eat a diet high in vitamins, omega-3 fatty acids, and antioxidants to support brain function.

- Maintain your intellectual curiosity by reading, going to classes, or taking up new interests.

- By increasing neuroplasticity and circulation, exercise benefits brain health.

Take pauses, relax, and engage in meditation. A happy mind is like a superhero cape for your brain, and a relaxed mind is a happy mind.

Preventive Steps Against Serious Illnesses

Let us now address the big bad wolves: diseases. Here, prevention is key to success.

- Get screened for diseases like diabetes, hypertension, and cancer.

- Make dietary changes to promote cardiovascular health, such as cutting back on sodium and saturated fat.

- Continue to exercise frequently to lower your risk of heart disease, obesity, and different types of cancer.

- To prevent skin cancer, use sunscreen, cover up with protective clothes, and limit your time outside in the sun.

- Reduce your exposure to tobacco products and give up smoking to lower your risk of respiratory and cardiovascular diseases.

- Drinking alcohol in moderation can help avoid liver and cardiac issues.

*****

Remember, it's not about living forever; it's about living well. It becomes clear as we negotiate the ups and downs of life that our journey is closely linked to the health of our body, mind, and spirit. Health is a whole state of thriving rather than just the absence of disease. Adopting a wealthy and health-conscious lifestyle requires deliberate decision-making, regular routines, and a dedication to general well-being. Allow each stride, each healthy meal, and each mindful moment to add to a life that is not only long but also incredibly full of health and energy.

Chapter 7: Navigating Through Stages of Life

Starting the journey through life's phases is similar to navigating a continuously shifting terrain because each stage brings with it unique lessons and opportunities to face mortality.

From Childhood to Adolescence: Initial Contacts with Death

Life is played out on the innocent playground at first. Childhood is a time for play, discovery, and blissful ignorance of death. However, we start to hear hints of life's transience even in the first few chapters. The concept of goodbye is first introduced by the death of a beloved pet, grandparent, or even fictional character.

The turbulent transitional period between childhood and adulthood, adolescence, heightens one's awareness of mortality. On the playgrounds, the sense of invincibility is challenged. The purpose of life, one's identity, and the certainty of death begin to take on a deeper meaning in one's thoughts. In order to prepare us for the resilience needed in the upcoming chapters, this stage transforms into a classroom where we start learning the profound lessons of life.

Developing Resilience from Young Adulthood

As we enter the stage of young adulthood, obstacles arise that call for perseverance. Now, the hopes and dreams sown in the soil of adolescence must contend with the harsh realities of life. Death is more than just an idea; it is a real force that can be felt when loved ones pass away or when the biological clock runs out.

Developing resilience takes center stage. Now is the time to mold how we react to the uncertainties of life. Our emotional strength is constructed through relationships that come and go, heartbreaks, and failures. Once a foreign concept, mortality now stands by our sides, encouraging us to live true lives and discover meaning in the midst of chaos.

Choosing Calm Above Anxiety in Old Age

We reach the pages of old age as the chapters progress. The body bears the marks of a life well lived, worn down by time. Death is now front and center, no longer a sidekick. The gradual passing of friends and personal losses serve as painful reminders of our limited time on earth.

However, at this point, there is a chance to choose calm over anxiety. The emphasis switches from being afraid of the running clock to savoring the time that is left. It is a time for introspection, giving thanks, and sharing the knowledge accumulated over a lifetime of experiences. Death turns into a friend, someone to be welcomed into a graceful acceptance of life's cycle rather than something to be feared.

In summary, innocence learns the hard lessons of mortality and lays the groundwork for future resilience. In this phase, resilience becomes the hero as mortality becomes a real force rather than just a concept. Old age, with its embrace of peace over worry, is an opportunity to pause, appreciate, and accept life's unavoidable circle with grace.

*****

Going through these phases is more than just traveling through time; it is a deep investigation of how mortality is changing our perspectives, our ability to bounce back from setbacks, and, in the end, how we live.

Chapter 8: Death Around Us

The threads of life and death intertwine in the vast tapestry of existence, occasionally broken by deep loss. This chapter covers the emotional journey of supporting a loved one through a terminal illness, explores the complex and delicate realms of bereavement, and highlights the powerful shared solace that communities can offer when faced with mortality.

Dealing with Bereavement and Loss

One common theme that runs through the story of human existence is the experience of loss. A loved one's departure due to death is similar to the breakdown of a meaningful relationship and leaves a lasting impression on the fabric of our lives. Grieving is a very personal process that goes through phases of loss, acceptance, and finally healing.

How Loss Affects Us

Loss has a profound effect on our emotional landscape, evoking a wide range of emotions. Common reactions include profound sadness, existential reflection, and a reassessment of the purpose of life. Furthermore, experiencing loss can lead to a feeling of loneliness, which can inspire contemplation of one's own mortality and a search for purpose following a significant absence.

How to Handle a Loss

Permit Yourself to Be Sad

Understand that grieving is a normal and essential process that attests to the depths of our relationships.

Look for Assistance

Be in the company of a network of understanding and consoling friends, family, or support groups.

Communicate Your Emotions

Find ways to express your feelings, whether it be through writing, art, or candid discussions with reliable people.

Honor and Remember

Establish memorials or rituals that celebrate and honor the lives of the deceased.

Expert Advice

To get professional assistance while navigating the complexities of grief, think about pursuing therapy or counseling.

Supporting Loved Ones through Terminal Illnesses

A diagnosis of a terminal illness not only changes the course of the life of the person facing death, but it also has an impact on those close to them. It demands a sobering contemplation of life's impermanence and a radical reassessment of viewpoints regarding death.

How It Affects Your Outlook on Life and Death

Being a rock of support for someone you love who is facing a terminal illness is an extremely emotional task. Experiencing their struggle can elicit a range of feelings, from profound compassion and empathy to fear and sorrow. It makes one reflect on the transience of life and emphasizes the value of savoring every moment that passes by. Taking care of a loved one who is close to death, however, can leave many with a severe fear of living again. The question "Will I too suffer like this and die one day?" may come up repeatedly, or "Will this disease also be inherited by me, and will it be the end of my days?"

Steps to Support and Cope

Open Communication

Encourage open and sincere dialogue about desires, fears, and the emotional roller coaster.

Seek Knowledge

Recognize the complexities of the condition and look into the resources that are available for all-encompassing assistance.

Prioritize Self-Care

Take care of your mental and emotional health, understanding that good help starts with a solid base.

Build a Support Network

Together with friends and family, divide up the workload to build a strong support network.

Prepare for the Future

Have conversations regarding final wishes and make the required preparations to ensure a more seamless transition.

Moving Forward

The journey continues into the aftermath after a loved one passes away. Grieving is a continuous process, and the departed's memories can inspire personal development and resilience. The bereaved person changes, walking a path where the possibility of significant transformation coexists with the resonance of loss.

Shared Solace—Communities Coming Together

Within the vast and frequently intimidating terrain of death, communities arise as guiding lights of mutual comfort, providing empathy and assistance. These communities, whether they exist in real or virtual spaces, foster settings where the fear of death is met with empathy and becomes a shared burden lessened by group strength.

How Communities Help Overcome Fear

Communities act as archives of common experiences, giving people a forum to freely express their loss. In these settings, the fear of dying is greeted with a sense of shared empathy that gradually turns it into a burden that is shared but made lighter by the strength of group support.

Ways in Which You Can Assist Others

Create Support Networks

Create or join communities where comfort and understanding are fostered by shared experiences.

Offer Compassion

Show compassion and understanding for bereaved individuals, fostering a space where feelings are freely shared.

Promote Open Conversations

Promote conversations about dying while eradicating the stigma and anxiety surrounding it.

Take Part in Customs

Participate in consensual rituals that provide comfort, fostering a sense of unity and humanity.

*****

The ability to navigate the deep depths of death around us calls for bravery, resiliency, and an understanding that comforting one another is a powerful way to combat fear of death. Although grieving and assisting loved ones with terminal illnesses are difficult experiences, they can be transformative and provide a valuable understanding of the complex fabric of life.

Facing these immense challenges helps us realize that death does not define us, even though it is inevitable. Rather, it becomes an essential component of the human experience as a whole, encouraging empathy, connections, and better comprehension of the complex dance between life and death. In shared solace, we discover that even in the face of loss, we are not alone.

Chapter 9: Practical Approaches to Discussing Death

It is impossible to overestimate the significance of having candid, open discussions about death as we navigate the complexities of mortality. Although talking about death is sometimes seen as a difficult and uncomfortable endeavor, it is an essential part of getting ready for the inevitable. This chapter looks at how to have the conversation about death in a practical way, how to deal with the awkwardness of talking about death, how to prepare for the end with funeral plans and wills, and how to help kids deal with the sensitive concept of mortality.

Having the Tough Discussions

Although having conversations about death can be difficult, they are essential for both practical and emotional preparedness. It takes tact and thought to start these conversations with parents, friends, partners, or professionals.

With Parents

Talking about death with parents can be a very sensitive topic. Start by letting them know you are willing to talk and stressing how important it is to respect their wishes. Be compassionate in your approach and give them space to express their preferences and ideas about end-of-life choices.

With Friends

Talking about it with friends requires a supportive atmosphere. Select a fitting location, be clear about your goals, and promote candid communication. Recognize that while talking about death can be uncomfortable, it is necessary to understand one another and approach the conversation with compassion.

With a Partner

Talking about death with a life partner is a deep and personal discussion. Commence by declaring your love and dedication, stressing that these conversations are evidence of your concern for each other's welfare. Share your thoughts on end-of-life preferences and encourage your partner to do the same.

With an Expert

Consulting with experts, such as end-of-life consultants, therapists, or estate planners, can yield insightful information. To ensure a fruitful and educational discussion, prepare for these talks by stating your concerns and objectives.

Initiating the Discussion

The desire for knowledge, comprehension, and readiness is what drives people to start having discussions about death. You can reduce anxiety and develop a sense of control over the unknown by talking about your fears, asking for help, and sharing your worries.

Having difficult conversations, especially ones concerning death, calls for consideration and compassion. These considerations try to promote candid and open communication by emphasizing the establishment of a supportive environment.

Selecting the appropriate environment is essential. Make sure there is privacy and a welcoming atmosphere that promotes candid conversation. The physical environment is very important in creating a secure environment for delicate discussions.

Being empathetic is just as important. Recognize the topic's inherent sensitivity and approach the discussion with empathy and understanding. Understanding the emotions at play facilitates communication and encourages a more sympathetic exchange of ideas and feelings.

In conversations about death, patience is a crucial quality. It is important to let the conversation flow naturally and to be aware that these exchanges might take some time. A patient approach gives people the freedom to think through and express themselves at their own speed.

The key is to promote transparency. Establish a space where everyone concerned can freely express their preferences, worries, and thoughts without worrying about being judged. Creating an environment of acceptance makes for a more sincere and real dialogue.

It makes sense to seek professional guidance when necessary. Experts like therapists or counselors can help steer the conversation and offer insightful information. Their knowledge and experience provide an extra degree of assistance and direction, particularly in difficult or delicate circumstances.

By taking these factors into account, the intention is to turn challenging conversations into chances for comprehension, empathy, and support; this will create an atmosphere where people feel free to express themselves and handle the subject of death with gentleness and understanding.

Planning for the End: Wills, Funerals, and Last Wishes

One delicate but essential component of responsible planning is thinking about death. Going beyond emotional talks, practical issues like creating a will—a legal document that specifies how property is divided and expresses final desires—become crucial. Making a thorough inventory of all assets, choosing a trustworthy executor, naming beneficiaries, and, if necessary, choosing guardians for dependents are all part of this process. Getting legal counsel guarantees that the will complies with all applicable laws.

Funeral plans give loved ones a roadmap, even though they are emotionally taxing. It is easier for those left behind to communicate preferences for prearranged services, budgetary considerations, ceremonial details, and options for cremation or burial. Expressing choices for memorialization, organ donation, and medical treatment are all part of communicating final wishes. Finally, keeping lines of communication open with loved ones regarding these factors facilitates a more seamless transition when the time comes. In acknowledging the inevitability of life's end, addressing these practical aspects fosters a sense of preparedness and consideration for those we leave behind.

Helping Children Understand Death

Because death is an abstract and complicated concept, talking about it with children requires a deliberate and cautious approach. Knowing that children have a hard time accepting that death is inevitable, the trick is knowing when and how to bring up this delicate topic.

Given that children generally begin to understand death more fully between the ages of seven and 10, it is important to modify conversations according to each person's maturity level rather than following a rigid age range.

Establish a peaceful, distraction-free atmosphere and explain topics using language that is appropriate for the child's age to help lead these conversations. Encourage kids to communicate their feelings and ask questions without worrying about being judged. It is crucial to strike a balance between giving assurance and being forthright about death's inevitable outcome.

Including media, books, movies, or television shows that delicately address the subject can also be a useful way to get conversations started. Through empathetic communication, transparency, and developmentally appropriate explanations, we can effectively navigate this delicate conversation with kids and build their understanding and support system.

*****

Managing conversations about death requires striking a careful balance between compassion, pragmatism, and empathy. People can cultivate a sense of preparedness, allay fears, and accept that mortality is inevitable by having hard talks, making funeral and will plans, and teaching children about death. By tackling these subjects head-on, we not only help ourselves but also foster a society that views death with candor, empathy, and understanding.

Chapter 10: Spiritual Practices to Connect with Mortality

Spiritual practices provide significant channels for connection, reflection, and comfort as we explore mortality. This chapter explores how engaging in spiritual activity can reduce fear and anxiety related to dying. These spiritual tools lead us on a journey of understanding and acceptance. They range from mindfulness exercises and meditation that help us stay in the present moment to prayer and faith-based practices that give us confidence and nature-based rituals that help us connect to life's cycle.

Meditation and Mindfulness Exercises

Mindfulness Meditation

Through the practice of mindfulness meditation, one can develop an acute awareness of the present moment and a strong bond with life. Here's a simple guide.

- Sit or lie down comfortably in a quiet space.

- Pay attention to your breath. Inhale and exhale slowly, grounding yourself in each breath.

- As thoughts arise, acknowledge them without judgment and gently guide your focus back to your breath.

- Gradually extend your awareness to sensations, sounds, and your surroundings, embracing the fullness of the present moment.

Loving-Kindness Meditation

Through the cultivation of compassion, this meditation promotes a positive perspective on life and relationships.

- Find a relaxed posture while sitting or lying down.

- Inhale and exhale, centering yourself in the present moment.

- Direct positive, loving thoughts toward yourself and others. Start with simple phrases like "May I/you be happy, may I/you be healthy."

- Gradually extend these wishes to friends, family, acquaintances, and even those you find challenging.

Body Scan Meditation

This practice involves focusing attention on different parts of the body, promoting relaxation and mindfulness.

- Find a quiet space and lie down on your back.

- Begin at your toes and slowly move upward, paying attention to each body part.

- If tension is detected, consciously relax that area. Continue scanning until you reach the top of your head.

- As you scan, synchronize your breath, inhaling calmness and exhaling tension.

Prayer and Faith-based Practices

Centering Prayer

Centering prayer is a contemplative practice that fosters spiritual connection and inner peace.

- Choose a word that holds personal spiritual significance.

- Sit comfortably, and close your eyes.

- Silently repeat the chosen word, allowing it to deepen your connection with the divine.

- When thoughts arise, gently return to the sacred word, embracing moments of silence.

Daily Gratitude Prayer

Expressing gratitude promotes positivity and a sense of abundance.

- Find a quiet space and take a few deep breaths.
- Acknowledge and reflect on the positive aspects of your life.
- Verbally or mentally, express gratitude for specific blessings.
- Conclude the prayer with positive intentions for the day.

Faith-based Scripture Reading

Use sacred texts to guide and reassure oneself spiritually.

- Choose verses that, as a Christian, Muslim, Hindu, or follower of any other religion, have significance for you.

- Make time for yourself in a calm, special place.

- Read the chosen scriptures slowly, stopping occasionally to consider their meanings.

- Take in the consolation and wisdom contained in the holy words.

Nature-based Rituals

Tree-Planting Ceremony

Planting a tree is a symbol of rebirth, development, and the everlasting cycle of nature.

- Decide on an appropriate location for the ceremony.

- Create a hole for the tree, bringing purpose to the work.

- After the tree is positioned in the hole, cover its roots with dirt.

- Think for a moment about the life cycle and acknowledge your connection to it.

Full Moon Meditation

Establishing a lunar cycle connection can provide a feeling of consistency and rhythm.

- Locate a spot where you can get a good view of the full moon.

- Take a comfortable seat or stand, and let the moonlight surround you.

- Consider the phases of the moon as a symbol of the fleeting nature of life.

- Declare with your words or in your mind that you want to live fully in the moment.

There are various practices that you could use to get in touch with your spiritual side and each one will help you build emotionally, becoming more adept at going through life daily without succumbing to the fear of death.

*****

By integrating these spiritual practices into our lives, we can establish meaningful connections with death. We can harness the transforming power of the spiritual realm to navigate our mortal journey with grace, understanding, and a profound sense of connection to the greater tapestry of existence by embracing mindfulness, prayer, and nature-based rituals.

Chapter 11: Inspirational Stories on Embracing Mortality

Stories are the threads that weave resiliency, inspiration, and hope throughout the fabric of the human experience. This chapter includes stories of people who, in the face of mortality, faced hardship with bravery and grace, overcame great obstacles in life, and became deeply inspirational despite their circumstances.

Living Fully in the Face of Terminal Illness

Facing a terminal illness can be a profound challenge, reshaping one's outlook on life. Overcoming such trials requires resilience and a commitment to living fully. Let's look at how Samantha, a vibrant soul diagnosed with a life-limiting condition, lived her life. Instead of succumbing to despair, she embraced each day with unyielding positivity.

Steps Samantha Took to Overcome Challenges

- She cultivated mindfulness to savor each moment.
- She fostered relationships that brought joy and support.
- She engaged in activities that ignited her spirit.
- She consulted with therapists and support groups.
- She focused on what brought her joy and fulfillment.

Samantha's story serves as a testament to the transformative power of living fully, emphasizing the importance of resilience and finding purpose even in the face of mortality.

Grief Transformed into Purpose and Action

Transforming grief into purpose is a powerful journey that reshapes one's perspective on life and death. A young man, Thomas, lost his mother in a sudden accident. It was unexpected, and the loss left him shocked; the grief was crippling. Eventually, he was back on his feet and trying to help others. He had discovered that he could channel his grief into meaningful action, creating positive change in his community.

Steps Thomas Took to Transform Grief

- He allowed himself to feel and express the pain of loss.
- He considered the values and causes that hold personal significance.
- Thomas channeled grief into actions that aligned with his values.
- He went on to connect with others who shared similar passions.
- Lastly, he acknowledged and celebrated the positive changes initiated.

Thomas' journey showcases the transformative potential of grief when channeled into purposeful action, demonstrating that even in the face of loss, one can contribute meaningfully to the world.

Inspiring Acts of Kindness and Generosity

Acts of generosity and kindness bridge the gap between life and death, leaving behind lasting legacies. Olivia, a middle-aged woman, believed that small acts could make a big difference. Her commitment to giving—whether through charitable contributions or small acts of kindness—showed a deep understanding of how interconnected everything is.

Steps Olivia Took to Practice Generosity

- She recognized moments of generosity in daily life.
- She understood the needs and feelings of others.

- She began with simple acts of kindness.
- She engaged in activities that benefited the community.
- She shared experiences to encourage generosity in others.

Olivia's legacy highlights the value of generosity in the human experience. It emphasizes how small deeds over time have a big impact and teach us to accept life as it is while giving assistance to those who are less fortunate and in need. This eliminates fear and anxiety, enabling you to move forward every day because of the meaning you have found in your life and the comfort you have given your soul.

*****

These uplifting tales are like notes of fortitude, bravery, and kindness in the eternal threads of human existence. People not only navigate the complexities of mortality but also add to a collective narrative of hope and shared humanity by practicing acts of kindness, embracing life in the face of terminal illness, and turning grief into purposeful action. These stories teach us that intentional and purposeful engagement with life's complex and ephemeral moments is just as important to living fully as avoiding death.

Chapter 12: Facing Our Own Mortality

We address the most intimate aspect of the journey—facing our own impending death—in the last chapter of our investigation into mortality. This chapter explores the transformative techniques that can result in a profound comprehension of the meaning embodied in the life-death cycle and a calm acceptance of mortality.

Overcoming Fear through Acceptance

Becoming aware of the value of acceptance is the first step toward overcoming the crippling fear of death. This journey is transformative; by accepting the unavoidable reality of our own transience, it opens the door to a more tranquil and fulfilling life.

Facing your fears head-on is an essential step on this acceptance journey. It takes reflection on your circumstances and an understanding of the root causes of your anxiety to identify and address specific fears associated with dying. This self-awareness turns into a major step toward accepting that death is inevitable.

The acceptance of impermanence is a crucial component of this journey. It means learning to see life's fleeting nature as a necessary component of its beauty rather than as a weakness. This change in viewpoint enables fear to be transformed into thankfulness, encouraging an appreciation for the fleeting moments that give life significance.

Finding one's life's purpose also relieves some of the tension associated with the journey's approaching end. You can experience a deep sense of fulfillment and purpose that lessens your fear of dying by taking a moment to reflect on the meaning and purpose you have given your life.

Additionally, developing mindfulness becomes an important tool for this journey. Engaging in mindfulness practices helps anchor one in the present moment, alleviating the fear associated with an uncertain future. By keeping one's attention on the present, worries about the future are reduced and a sense of comfort is found in the experience.

This all-encompassing strategy, which is intertwined with mindfulness and introspection, acts as a reassuring guide, converting fear into a greater understanding of the fleeting beauty that is inherent in the human experience.

The Power of Forgiveness—To Others and Yourself

The practice of forgiveness is a useful tactic for getting over the fear of dying. Forgiveness does more than just improve mental health; it also gives us closure, releases us from the weight of grudges, and makes us feel better emotionally.

Thinking back on past wrongs becomes an essential first step in the process of forgiving others. Compiling a list of unspoken grievances and resentments enables one to consciously recognize that forgiveness is a powerful gift to oneself rather than an endorsement of others' actions. It establishes the foundation for the transformational procedure.

Developing empathy is a crucial step on the path to forgiveness. Putting oneself in the shoes of people who may have harmed others can increase empathy and pave the way for comprehension and, eventually, forgiveness.

Making the conscious choice to pardon is a big step forward. Emotional healing is aided by the decision to forgive those who have wronged us and, as important, by forgiving oneself for any perceived shortcomings or regrets.

It is acknowledged that forgiving someone else can be a difficult process, so getting help is advised. If managing complicated emotions proves to be challenging, seeking advice from a therapist or counselor can be a helpful tool in helping the forgiveness process along.

This method, which views forgiveness as a potent instrument, offers a great sense of release from the burden of resentment, in addition to a way to achieve emotional healing and closure and lessen the fear of dying.

Dying Well—Peaceful Transitioning

Dying well is more than just the physical act of passing away; it also includes embracing the process with composure, dignity, and a feeling of achievement. For a peaceful transition, the journey toward its inevitable end must be prioritized in terms of quality.

Making end-of-life plans is a fundamental step in promoting a peaceful transition. Giving instructions to those left behind about your final wishes for funeral and medical arrangements is a helpful parting gift. Clarity and agreement with your wishes are ensured when these plans are shared with those you love.

It becomes crucial to have meaningful conversations. Sharing your ideas, emotions, and wishes with close friends or family members helps you and the people you love feel less emotionally strained. Good communication is essential to creating a supportive and understanding environment.

Focusing on legacy is an additional significant facet of peaceful transitioning. Think about the kind of legacy you want to leave behind—whether that be through preserving memories, sharing knowledge, or contributing to causes that are important to you. It is this focus that gives the transition a purpose.

Taking up spiritual activities helps one feel at ease and at peace. Take part in spiritual practices that are consistent with your beliefs; these practices could be meditation, prayer, or rituals. Throughout the process of transition, these practices act as anchors, bringing peace and comfort.

By incorporating these stages, the method for peaceful transitioning provides a comprehensive viewpoint, highlighting the importance of not just the physical act of passing away but also the relational, emotional, and spiritual aspects that influence the journey's quality.

*****

The journey transcends fear as we come to terms with our own mortality and becomes an investigation of acceptance, forgiveness, and a gentle transition. Through accepting transience, forgiving, and getting ready for a peaceful end, we light the way to a peaceful resolution. We find the ability to live fully, love deeply, and leave a legacy that endures beyond the confines of time when we accept our own mortality.

Conclusion

We stand at the intersection of reflection and acceptance as we wrap up our investigation into the complex fabric of mortality. Although death is sometimes perceived as a terrifying abyss, it actually serves as a profound mirror that reflects the essence of our existence. This book has been a voyage through the intertwined strands of spirituality and faith, revealing how they influence our understanding of life's ultimate end. In a society where dying is frequently dreaded, misinterpreted, or avoided, our comprehension grows as we accept death as a necessary component of life's journey rather than as its conclusion. Recognizing one's own mortality does not imply a morbid obsession with dying; rather, it is a step toward a deeper appreciation of each breath and each heartbeat.

Key Takeaways

An Inseparable Bond

Knowing oneself to be mortal is like looking down into an infinite chasm. It is a multifaceted, illuminating journey where all cultures and religions offer distinctive viewpoints on death, providing us with a diverse range of beliefs. These convictions, which are intertwined with spirituality and faith, help us understand the profound influence of mortality on our lives.

Faith and Spirituality as Lenses

Spirituality and faith serve as more than just coping mechanisms for grief; they are prisms through which we view and comprehend life. Our choices, moral judgments, and interpersonal interactions are shaped by our beliefs about the afterlife, which ultimately determine who we are.

Comfort in Belief Systems

Our convictions give us solace and direction when faced with the inevitable. Regardless of their stance on religion or atheism, people derive comfort and purpose from their own perspectives on death. These various belief systems serve as pillars, encouraging us to treasure every moment and providing hope when it seems to be lacking.

Real-World Resilience

Steve Jobs' belief that death can be a transformative force and Viktor Frankl's fortitude in the face of the Holocaust serve as examples of how faith can give meaning to life even in the face of hardship. These incidents highlight how spirituality can help people deal with the most difficult situations in life.

Scientific Validation

The strong correlation between religious beliefs and attitudes regarding death has been confirmed by numerous studies. It is impossible to overstate the significant influence that spirituality has on coping strategies and psychological health.

Cultural Perspectives

Diversity in culture deepens our comprehension of death. Various traditions—including Judaism, Christianity, Islam, Buddhism, and Hinduism—have different perspectives on death, which add depth to our study and help us recognize the diversity of human viewpoints.

We have discovered through our investigation of mortality that accepting life is inextricably linked to realizing and accepting our own mortality. It is important to acknowledge death as a necessary component of life's symphony rather than giving up on it. This acceptance acts as a potent catalyst for concentrating on living truly, savoring each moment, and overcoming obstacles in life with fortitude and purpose.

- Do not forget that accepting your mortality is a step toward a greater appreciation of life itself rather than a path toward an obsession with death. We can appreciate the depth of every experience by changing our viewpoint.

- Thinking about death makes one less interested in material things and more inclined toward altruism. As we become more aware of life's fleeting nature, we prioritize making meaningful connections and contributions.

- Accepting our death turns into a liberating experience that helps us live more truly. We are free to pursue what really matters when we accept that our existence is limited.

- Embracing our mortality turns into a powerful anxiety-reduction strategy that promotes better lifestyle choices. It's an invitation to live mindfully, free from the shackles of fear.

- It can be transforming to acknowledge your fear and work toward accepting death as a normal part of life. It is a path that leads to lives that are happier and more meaningful, where each breath turns into a celebration of the blessing of life.

Embracing mortality becomes the melody that harmonizes our journey, leading us to not just traverse but truly live in the grand symphony of life and death. Let us keep these words in mind as we make our way toward the unknown destination that is mortality:

"Death is not extinguishing the light; it is simply putting out the lamp because the dawn has come." -Rabindranath Tagore (*Rabindranath Tagore Quotes*, n.d.)

References

A quote from The Power of Now. (n.d.). Goodreads. Retrieved January 24, 2024, from https://www.goodreads.com/quotes/1339392-the-secret-of-life-is-to-die-before-you-die

Albert Einstein Quotes. (n.d.). BrainyQuote. https://www.brainyquote.com/quotes/albert_einstein_161289

Isaac Asimov Quotes. (n.d.). BrainyQuote. https://www.brainyquote.com/quotes/isaac_asimov_103611

Rabindranath Tagore Quotes. (n.d.). BrainyQuote. https://www.brainyquote.com/quotes/rabindranath_tagore_386459

Did you love *LIVING WITH DEATH*? Then you should read *BETRAYAL - NOT EVERYONE IS A FRIEND*[1] by SHY HOUSTON!

Book Description

Have you ever lost a close friend? Someone you thought you would be best friends with for life?

If so, you're in the same boat as almost everybody. We've all been burned by someone we once called a friend, and it's no exaggeration to say that it can be heartbreaking.

It is estimated that by the time we hit our thirties, many of us can count our close friends on one hand.

---

1. https://books2read.com/u/4E7X7A

2. https://books2read.com/u/4E7X7A

That is because people have enough time to show their true colors and intentions. So, when this does inevitably happen, how should you react? And how can you prevent it from occurring in the future?

Within the pages of Betrayal—Not Everyone Is a Friend, you will gain access to comprehensive solutions to all the issues that can arise from a close friend's deception, broken promises, and betrayal.

This book will help you identify a wolf in sheep's clothing before they can truly hurt you while also offering you all the tools and strategies to deal with the aftermath of getting burned by someone close to you.

Inside Betrayal—Not Everyone Is a Friend, discover:

The true impact of broken promises and how to identify the problems before they arise.

A deeper understanding of what drives someone to betray someone close to them.

Ways to live with the fallout of deceit.

The unwavering importance of trust in any relationship.

How to heal from betrayal.

It's important to gain the insight you need to overcome getting betrayed and learn how to prevent this from happening again in the future.

Grab your copy of Betrayal—Not Everyone Is a Friend today!

Read more at https://www.amazon.com/author/shyhouston.

About the Author

I am a daughter, sister, wife and mother. The most important thing in my life is my husband, kids and family. I am Irish born and emigrated to New York in 1986. I built a life here with my husband and we were blessed with three sons. While I spent my career working with figures in the accounting realm, I always had a passion for writing. Having experienced many challenges throughout my life, I am hoping my writing can help others navigate their own path by raising awareness about important issues.

Read more at https://www.amazon.com/author/shyhouston.